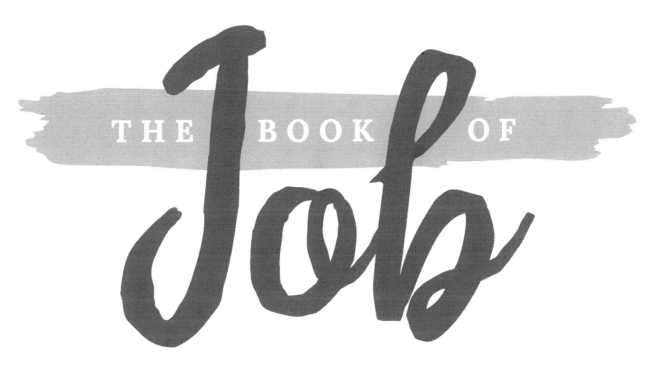

THE BOOK OF Job

ONE CHAPTER A DAY

GoodMorningGirls.org

The Book of Job

Welcome to Good Morning Girls! We are so glad you are joining us.

God created us to walk with Him, to know Him, and to be loved by Him. He is our living well, and when we drink from the water He continually provides, His living water will change the entire course of our lives.

Jesus said: "Whoever drinks of the water that I will give him will never be thirsty again. The water that I will give him will become in him a spring of water welling up to eternal life." ~ John 4:14 (ESV)

So let's begin.

The method we use here at GMG is called the **SOAK** method.

- ❑ **S**—The S stands for *Scripture*—Read the chapter for the day. Then choose 1-2 verses and write them out word for word. (There is no right or wrong choice—just let the Holy Spirit guide you.)

- ❑ **O**—The O stands for *Observation*—Look at the verse or verses you wrote out. Write 1 or 2 observations. What stands out to you? What do you learn about the character of God from these verses? Is there a promise, command or teaching?

- ❑ **A**—The A stands for *Application*—Personalize the verses. What is God saying to you? How can you apply them to your life? Are there any changes you need to make or an action to take?

- ❑ **K**—The K stands for *Kneeling in Prayer*—Pause, kneel and pray. Confess any sin God has revealed to you today. Praise God for His word. Pray the passage over your own life or someone you love. Ask God to help you live out your applications.

SOAK God's word into your heart and squeeze every bit of nourishment you can out of each day's scripture reading. Soon you will find your life transformed by the renewing of your mind!

Walk with the King!

Courtney

WomenLivingWell.org, GoodMorningGirls.org

Join the GMG Community

Share your daily SOAK at 7:45am on **Facebook.com/GoodMorningGirlsWLW**

Instagram: WomenLivingWell #GoodMorningGirls

GMG Bible Coloring Chart

COLORS	KEYWORDS
PURPLE	God, Jesus, Holy Spirit, Saviour, Messiah
PINK	women of the Bible, family, marriage, parenting, friendship, relationships
RED	love, kindness, mercy, compassion, peace, grace
GREEN	faith, obedience, growth, fruit, salvation, fellowship, repentance
YELLOW	worship, prayer, praise, doctrine, angels, miracles, power of God, blessings
BLUE	wisdom, teaching, instruction, commands
ORANGE	prophecy, history, times, places, kings, genealogies, people, numbers, covenants, vows, visions, oaths, future
BROWN/GRAY	Satan, sin, death, hell, evil, idols, false teachers, hypocrisy, temptation

Introduction to the Book of Job

The book of Job was born out of pain. In all that Job went through, he never cursed God, even when his wife told him to. His friends came to give "encouragement" that turned into a time of questioning Jobs character and actions. There is much we can learn as we examine the life of Job, and how we react when hard times come.

Purpose: The book of Job teaches us how to endure through suffering and addresses the question of "why do the righteous suffer". Suffering will come to all in this world, but we see that Job does not curse God and we should not either. The book of Job also shows the relationship between God and man and how we need to respond with faith and trust in God's sovereign grace.

Author: Unknown

Date: Job is the oldest book of the Bible, although the exact dates are unknown. Based on context, it seems to be pre-mosaic, even patriarchal from the second millennium B.C.

Key verse: The Lord gave, and the Lord has taken away; blessed be the name of the Lord. Job 1:21

Why do the righteous suffer? Why do bad things happen to good people?

The book of Job gives us this insight. We live in a broken world and as a result bad things are going to happen – even to good people. However, people have always believed that these go hand in hand with sin. While this is true at times, it is not always the case.

The book of Job brings comfort to those who are going through hard times because they can relate to the main character of the story.

Major Themes of the Book of Job:

1. Our loyalty to God should not be based on our prosperity. If we are only loyal to God when blessings flow – that is a shallow faith. (Job 1:9-10)

2. When bad things happen in our lives, it is important to acknowledge that God is sovereign over all, whether it is good or bad. (Job 1:20-21)

3. God is the creator and sustainer of all things. Failure to acknowledge God's role in our lives, reduces our perspective and sets us up for spiritual struggles. (Job 38:36)

4. Satan will attack. Satan tries to draw a wedge between God and Job. We must recognize that Satan tries to attack us and drive a wedge between God and us. We must not allow this to happen.

A Layout of the Book:

    1. Job's Distress (1-3)

    2. Job's Defense (4-37)

    3. Job's Deliverance (38-42)

Job shows us that suffering is going to happen. It is how we suffer that will testify of our relationship with the Lord.

Do we blame God in our suffering, or do we see Him as sovereign and know that He is still good?

Do we trust the words of our friends, or lean into the very presence and Word of God?

It is easy to think we have the answers. Only God truly does. Bad things are going to happen - and when they do, we need to rest in the sovereign arms of our loving God.

The book of Job is going to ask us to evaluate the hard times in our lives and see them through eternal eyes. May we let the wisdom of the Lord invade our thoughts, even in the hardest places of our lives.

The Lord gave,

and the Lord has taken away;

blessed be the name of the Lord.

Job 1:21

Reflection Question:

It's easy to praise and follow God in the good times.

How can you remember to remain faithful in the bad times as well?

S—The S stands for *Scripture*

O—The O stands for *Observation*

A—The A stands for *Application*

K—The K stands for *Kneeling in Prayer*

Shall we receive good from God,

and shall we not receive evil?"

In all this Job did not sin with his lips.

Job 2:10

Reflection Question:

Have you ever had a time in your life when someone has encouraged you to walk away from God?

How did you respond?

S—The S stands for *Scripture*

O—The O stands for *Observation*

A—The A stands for *Application*

K—The K stands for *Kneeling in Prayer*

I am not at ease,

Nor am I quiet;

I have no rest,

but trouble comes.

Job 3:26

Reflection Question:

We have all had times when we've questioned why it is we must deal with certain things.

How has God shown you comfort in those times?

S—The S stands for *Scripture*

O—The O stands for *Observation*

A—The A stands for *Application*

K—The K stands for *Kneeling in Prayer*

Your words have upheld

him who was stumbling,

and you have made firm

the feeble knees.

Job 4:4

Reflection Question:

Sometimes when we are faced with trials, it is hard to remember that God will not desert us.

How do you remain focused on God, during difficult seasons of life?

S—The S stands for *Scripture*

O—The O stands for *Observation*

A—The A stands for *Application*

K—The K stands for *Kneeling in Prayer*

Behold, blessed is the one

whom God reproves;

therefore despise not the discipline

of the Almighty.

Job 5:17

Reflection Question:

We are reminded today, that when God disciplines us, we are in fact blessed.

How can we find the silver lining in difficult moments? Name a time when you have had to do so.

S—The S stands for *Scripture*

O—The O stands for *Observation*

A—The A stands for *Application*

K—The K stands for *Kneeling in Prayer*

Teach me,

and I will be silent;

make me understand

how I have gone astray.

Job 6:24

Reflection Question:

Job earnestly wants to know what he has done wrong and the lessons he needs to pull from this.

Name a time when you struggled to find what God was trying to show you.

S—The S stands for *Scripture*

O—The O stands for *Observation*

A—The A stands for *Application*

K—The K stands for *Kneeling in Prayer*

What is man,

that you make so much of him,

and that you set your heart on him?

Job 7:17

Reflection Question:

Job is uncertain about his purpose in life because he is unable to see the big picture.

Have you taken the time to discuss with God what your purpose is? What has He shown you?

Job 7

S—The S stands for *Scripture*

O—The O stands for *Observation*

A—The A stands for *Application*

K—The K stands for *Kneeling in Prayer*

Behold, God will not

reject a blameless man,

nor take the hand of evildoers.

Job 8:20

Reflection Question:

Bildad accused Job of having some sort of secret sin.

Have you ever been quick to judge someone? How can you make that right?

Job 8

S—The S stands for **Scripture**

O—The O stands for **Observation**

A—The A stands for **Application**

K—The K stands for **Kneeling in Prayer**

[God] is wise in heart and mighty in strength—

who has hardened himself against

him, and succeeded?

Job 9:4

Reflection Question:

It's easy to become discouraged when we feel we are doing everything right and bad things still continue to happen.

What are some ways that you can gain encouragement in those moments?

S—The S stands for *Scripture*

O—The O stands for *Observation*

A—The A stands for *Application*

K—The K stands for *Kneeling in Prayer*

You have granted me life and steadfast love, and your care has preserved my spirit.

Job 10:12

Reflection Question:

It's easy to allow discouragement to turn into bitterness and self-pity.

Share a verse that provides you with hope and encouragement in those difficult moments.

Job 10

S—The S stands for *Scripture*

O—The O stands for *Observation*

A—The A stands for *Application*

K—The K stands for *Kneeling in Prayer*

You will forget your misery;

You will remember it as waters

That have passed away.

Job 11:16

Reflection Question:

Even in our darkest moments there is always hope.

Name a time when you have found hope in the midst of a dark moment.

S—The S stands for *Scripture*

O—The O stands for *Observation*

A—The A stands for *Application*

K—The K stands for *Kneeling in Prayer*

With God are wisdom and might;

He has counsel and understanding.

Job 12:13

Reflection Question:

We have been reminded just how powerful God truly is.

How does this bring encouragement to you?

S—The S stands for **Scripture**

O—The O stands for **Observation**

A—The A stands for **Application**

K—The K stands for **Kneeling in Prayer**

Though he slay me,

I will hope in him.

Job 13:15

Reflection Question:

There will always be those who question your Christian walk.

How do you handle those types of situations?

Job 13

S—The S stands for ***Scripture***

O—The O stands for ***Observation***

A—The A stands for ***Application***

K—The K stands for ***Kneeling in Prayer***

Man who is born of a woman

is few of days and full of trouble.

Job 14:1

Reflection Question:

Everything in this world has an end. Yet, we have the assurance that through our salvation, even our earthly death is not the end.

How do these words of truth bring you comfort?

S—The S stands for *Scripture*

O—The O stands for *Observation*

A—The A stands for *Application*

K—The K stands for *Kneeling in Prayer*

For the company

of the godless

is barren.

Job 15:34

Reflection Question:

Everyone's Christian walk looks different. Because of this, there will always be those who question your actions.

How can you break this trend by being an encouragement to a fellow Christian who may be going through the same kind of judgment?

S—The S stands for *Scripture*

O—The O stands for *Observation*

A—The A stands for *Application*

K—The K stands for *Kneeling in Prayer*

My witness is in heaven,

and he who testifies for me

is on high.

Job 16:19

Reflection Question:

Job is realizing he has surrounded himself with those who are not compassionate and who are unwilling to provide comfort.

Do you have relationships like this in your own life?

S—The S stands for *Scripture*

O—The O stands for *Observation*

A—The A stands for *Application*

K—The K stands for *Kneeling in Prayer*

Yet the righteous
holds to his way,
and he who has clean hands
grows stronger and stronger.

Job 17:9

Reflection Question:

Job is feeling as though all the people in his life have turned their backs on him.

Has there been a relationship in your life that you have felt as though the person turned their back on you? How did you overcome the hurt?

S—The S stands for *Scripture*

O—The O stands for *Observation*

A—The A stands for *Application*

K—The K stands for *Kneeling in Prayer*

The light of the wicked

is put out,

and the flame of his fire

does not shine.

Job 18:5

Reflection Question:

Bildad originally started out trying to be an encouragement (Job 8). However, he has lost his patience and has become yet another discouragement.

Name a time when you stumbled at encouraging someone and instead became a discouragement.

S—The S stands for *Scripture*

O—The O stands for *Observation*

A—The A stands for *Application*

K—The K stands for *Kneeling in Prayer*

For I know

that my Redeemer lives,

and at the last

He will stand upon the earth.

Job 19:25

Reflection Question:

Even though Job is discouraged, he takes comfort in the fact that his redeemer lives.

How does remembering this, bring you comfort in your own day to day struggles?

S—The S stands for *Scripture*

O—The O stands for *Observation*

A—The A stands for *Application*

K—The K stands for *Kneeling in Prayer*

The exulting of the wicked is short,

and the joy of the godless

but for a moment.

Job 20:5

Reflection Question:

The life and pleasure of the wicked is temporary. Sin ruins feelings of joy and happiness.

How can you ensure that this simple truth doesn't play out in your own life?

Job 20

S—The S stands for *Scripture*

O—The O stands for *Observation*

A—The A stands for *Application*

K—The K stands for *Kneeling in Prayer*

Will any teach God knowledge,

seeing that he judges

those who are on high?

Job 21:22

Reflection Question:

Sometimes it is easy to get discouraged when you feel as though the wicked are prospering.

In what ways can you remain focused on God, instead of on how others are benefiting from wrongful actions?

S—The S stands for *Scripture*

O—The O stands for *Observation*

A—The A stands for *Application*

K—The K stands for *Kneeling in Prayer*

If you return to the Almighty

you will be built up.

Job 22:23

Reflection Question:

Have you ever been in the midst of a spiritual battle and had friends make accusations about your relationship with God being the issue?

If so, how did you respond to the accusations?

Job 22

S—The S stands for *Scripture*

O—The O stands for *Observation*

A—The A stands for *Application*

K—The K stands for *Kneeling in Prayer*

But he knows the way that I take;

when he has tried me,

I shall come out as gold.

Job 23:10

Reflection Question:

Job knew God was working on him through these trials. He did not doubt God.

When you're faced with trials, how do you keep your faith strong and remain close to the Lord?

S—The S stands for *Scripture*

O—The O stands for *Observation*

A—The A stands for *Application*

K—The K stands for *Kneeling in Prayer*

There are those

who rebel against the light,

who are not acquainted with its ways,

and do not stay in its paths.

Job 24:13

Reflection Question:

Job's friends tried to say he was being punished because he was being wicked, but Job's response reminds them that God's judgments aren't always seen.

How have you seen this to be true throughout your life?

S—The S stands for **Scripture**

O—The O stands for **Observation**

A—The A stands for **Application**

K—The K stands for **Kneeling in Prayer**

Dominion and fear are with God;

He makes peace in his high heaven.

Job 25:2

Reflection Question:

God is so much more than we could ever imagine and we can never compare to Him.

How do you keep in mind the holiness of God versus the sinful, human nature of man?

S—The S stands for ***Scripture***

O—The O stands for ***Observation***

A—The A stands for ***Application***

K—The K stands for ***Kneeling in Prayer***

He stretches out the north

over the void and

hangs the earth on nothing.

Job 26:7

Reflection Question:

God's ways most certainly are higher than our ways.

What power of God have you seen in your life that left you speechless and in awe of Him?

Job 26

S—The S stands for *Scripture*

O—The O stands for *Observation*

A—The A stands for *Application*

K—The K stands for *Kneeling in Prayer*

My lips will not speak falsehood,

and my tongue will not utter deceit.

Job 27:4

Reflection Question:

Job refuses to speak out against his friends, who spoke out against him, because of his integrity.

How have you kept your integrity with friends that have spoken out against you?

S—The S stands for ***Scripture***

O—The O stands for ***Observation***

A—The A stands for ***Application***

K—The K stands for ***Kneeling in Prayer***

The fear of the Lord,

is wisdom,

and to turn away from evil

is understanding.

Job 28:28

Reflection Question:

In order to gain wisdom and understanding, we must fear the Lord and depart from evil.

What steps are you taking to pursue wisdom and understanding in your life?

Job 28

S—The S stands for *Scripture*

O—The O stands for *Observation*

A—The A stands for *Application*

K—The K stands for *Kneeling in Prayer*

I put on righteousness,

and it clothed me.

Job 29:14

Reflection Question:

Job walked with the Lord and touched the lives of many in his lifetime and beyond.

How has Job's testimony impacted your life?

S—The S stands for *Scripture*

O—The O stands for *Observation*

A—The A stands for *Application*

K—The K stands for *Kneeling in Prayer*

And now my soul
is poured out within me;
days of affliction
have taken hold of me.

Job 30:16

Reflection Question:

Job served the Lord and others faithfully, but trials still came his way.

Have you had a similar experience? If so, in what ways did you continue growing in the Lord throughout the process?

S—The S stands for *Scripture*

O—The O stands for *Observation*

A—The A stands for *Application*

K—The K stands for *Kneeling in Prayer*

Let me be weighted

in a just balance,

and let God know my integrity!

Job 31:6

Reflection Question:

Job speaks out to clear himself from the false accusations of his friends.

If you were in Job's situation how would you have attempted to clear your name and still give glory to God as Job did?

S—The S stands for *Scripture*

O—The O stands for *Observation*

A—The A stands for *Application*

K—The K stands for *Kneeling in Prayer*

I will not show

partiality to any man

or use flattery

toward any person.

Job 32:21

Reflection Question:

Elihu waited until the elder friends of Job spoke before speaking. He chose to honor them in this way.

Do you take time to listen to what your spiritual elders have to say before you speak?

Job 32

S—The S stands for *Scripture*

O—The O stands for *Observation*

A—The A stands for *Application*

K—The K stands for *Kneeling in Prayer*

Then man prays to God,

and he accepts him;

he sees his face with a shout of joy,

and he restores to man his righteousness.

Job 33:26

Reflection Question:

Elihu recognizes God's grace, mercy and mediation for those who have sinned.

How have you experienced God's grace and mercy in your life?

S—The S stands for *Scripture*

O—The O stands for *Observation*

A—The A stands for *Application*

K—The K stands for *Kneeling in Prayer*

God will not do wickedly,

and the Almighty

will not pervert justice.

Job 34:12

Reflection Question:

Elihu spoke kindly and pointed to God, His character and His ways, while speaking to Job of his errors.

When someone approaches you and points to God throughout their correction, how do you receive them?

S—The S stands for *Scripture*

O—The O stands for *Observation*

A—The A stands for *Application*

K—The K stands for *Kneeling in Prayer*

Look at the heavens, and see;

and behold the clouds,

which are higher than you.

Job 35:5

Reflection Question:

Living through trials can cause us to say things we don't mean or that we regret later.

How have you responded through the midst of the trials in your life? Do you have any regrets and what can you learn from them?

S—The S stands for *Scripture*

O—The O stands for *Observation*

A—The A stands for *Application*

K—The K stands for *Kneeling in Prayer*

Behold, God is mighty.

Job 36:5

Reflection Question:

Often, our trials will not conclude until we've learned the lesson God has for us.

Are you in a trial right now? What lesson is God teaching you through it?

Job 36

S—The S stands for *Scripture*

O—The O stands for *Observation*

A—The A stands for *Application*

K—The K stands for *Kneeling in Prayer*

God thunders wondrously

with his voice;

He does great things

that we cannot comprehend.

Job 37:5

Reflection Question:

When we consider the wonders of God, we realize how truly insignificant we are without Him in our lives.

How can you keep God first in your life to help you remain humble?

Job 37

S—The S stands for **Scripture**

O—The O stands for **Observation**

A—The A stands for **Application**

K—The K stands for **Kneeling in Prayer**

Then the LORD answered Job
out of the whirlwind and said:
"Who is this that darkens counsel
by words without knowledge?"

Job 38:1,2

Reflection Question:

When God steps in to correct us, He often reminds us of how little we truly know.

Has God attempted to correct you recently? If so, in what way and how have you responded?

Job 38

S—The S stands for *Scripture*

O—The O stands for *Observation*

A—The A stands for *Application*

K—The K stands for *Kneeling in Prayer*

"Is it by your understanding that the hawk soars and spreads his wings toward the south?

Is it at your command that the eagle mounts up and makes his nest on high?"

Job 39:26,27

Reflection Question:

Often we need to be reminded just how amazing God's creation is and that without Him, we can do nothing.

What part of creation causes you to be filled with awe and humility?

Job 39

S—The S stands for *Scripture*

O—The O stands for *Observation*

A—The A stands for *Application*

K—The K stands for *Kneeling in Prayer*

Have you an arm like God,

and can you thunder

with a voice like his?

Job 40:9

Reflection Question:

God confronts Job because of the state of his heart and the words he had spoken against Him.

Share a time when God confronted you because of the state of your heart and words you had spoken.

S—The S stands for *Scripture*

O—The O stands for *Observation*

A—The A stands for *Application*

K—The K stands for *Kneeling in Prayer*

Who has first given to me,

that I should repay him?

Whatever is under the whole

heaven is mine.

Job 41:11

Reflection Question:

Everything belongs to God. We must never forget the depth of this truth.

How do you remember that nothing truly belongs to you, and that all has been given to us, by God?

S—The S stands for *Scripture*

O—The O stands for *Observation*

A—The A stands for *Application*

K—The K stands for *Kneeling in Prayer*

The Lord blessed
the latter days of Job
more than his beginning.

Job 42:12

Reflection Question:

After Job's trials, corrections, and repentance, abundant blessings came from the Lord.

Have you taken time to acknowledge the blessings you have received from God, following the trials in your life?

Job 42

S—The S stands for **Scripture**

O—The O stands for **Observation**

A—The A stands for **Application**

K—The K stands for **Kneeling in Prayer**

Special Thanks

I want to extend a special thank you to Mandy Kelly, Rosilind Jukic, Bridget Childress and Misty Leask for your help with this journal. Your love, dedication and leadership to the Good Morning Girls ministry is such a blessing to all. Thank you for giving to the Lord.

~ Courtney

Made in the USA
Lexington, KY
10 June 2016